Three Retrievers'

Guide to F

Your Lost Cat

By James Branson

ISBN-13: 978-1489577870

ISBN-10: 1489577874

I lost my favorite cat in 1997. He meant the world to me, and I didn't know what to do. I checked the shelter, put up fliers, and talked to my neighbors. We received a few sightings that turned out to be the wrong cat. After many months, I gradually gave up looking. It wasn't until years later that I learned how to search properly for a lost cat. In 2008, I took my Three Retrievers, Porter, Tess, and Kelsy, to the local off-leash park for some horseplay, and I saw a flier about training your dog to find lost dogs and cats. Instantly, I knew that was what I wanted to do with my youngest dog, Kelsy. Kelsy and I spent four years volunteering with Missing Pet Partnership, under the guidance of Kat Albrecht, a pioneer of many techniques for finding lost pets. Last year, I accidentally acquired a mutt named Komu, who turned out to be the best cat-finding dog I've ever worked with. In the past four years, through training and experience, I've learned what works and what doesn't, when you are looking for a cat. I learned that I had taken the wrong approach in 1997, and I had missed many opportunities that might have led me to my cat, Charlie.

If your cat is missing, you want to get out there and do something, not read a handbook. However, what you don't know could greatly reduce your chances of finding your cat. This information might take about an hour to read, and it could save you many hours of looking the wrong way. Learning the right approach will allow you to focus your energies on the strategies most likely to succeed. On the internet, and passed through the grapevine, a massive amount of misinformation is waiting to distract you from proper search methods. People believe these odd claims and well-meaning tips because they don't have a wealth of experience to draw from. With this book, you do have my years of experience to guide you, so you don't have to make the same mistakes that people have been making for years. In the company of Komu and several other cat-detection dogs, I have been intimately involved in the searches for dozens of cats. I have provided consultations on hundreds of other missing cat cases. I have witnessed what works and what does not. You can benefit from this experience and avoid the mistakes I made when I lost my cat. You can also find additional help at the Three Retrievers Lost Pet Rescue web site, www.3retrievers.com

What not to do:

1. Don't panic.
2. Don't wait.
3. Don't believe everything people tell you.
4. Don't call the name of a lost cat.
5. Don't give up.

Steps to take. (These steps are listed in the order most useful for the typical lost cat. Your case may require a different approach.)

1. Check thoroughly inside the house and garage.
2. Enlist help.
3. Keep a written record of everything.
4. Understand lost cat behavior.
5. Protect yourself.
6. Print fliers.
7. Mark the rear window of your car.
8. Ask the neighbors.
9. Create large neon posters.
10. Check the shelters.
11. Look in the right places, at the right times.
12. Use social media and internet tools.
13. Use a cat-detection dog, if available.
14. Use a vocal cat to attract the missing cat.
15. Consider an automated calling service.
16. Use a wildlife camera.
17. Set a trap.

What not to do.

1. Don't panic.

You may not even realize your cat is missing at first. You might assume he is sleeping in the back bedroom, or exploring the neighbor's yard. Eventually, when he misses dinner or doesn't paw at the door at the expected time, you will realize he is not where he is supposed to be. This realization can trigger a wave of panic that paralyzes, that clouds your mind and makes you feel utterly helpless. Taking positive steps toward finding your cat will improve your odds of finding him, but it will also channel your energies and focus your thoughts, freeing you from the grip of panic. Although the situation certainly may be an emergency from your cat's perspective, all emergencies have best practices and procedures that increase the odds of a good outcome. With medical, fire, and police emergencies, established procedures help emergency personnel provide the most effective response. In the case of your lost cat, you will be the first responder, probably, and the primary emergency manager. Although you can get help from a trained volunteer or professional, chances are such an expert won't be available just when you need one. Following the steps outlined here, as best you can, will give you positive actions to take and help you minimize or avoid that crippling feeling of panic.

2. Don't wait.

If you are like me, and your cats and dogs mean the world to you, you will feel as if your child is missing. Not everyone shares this view. When you begin to search, you may well encounter opinions telling you just to wait. People will tell you stories of cats that came home after a few days or a week. It is true that cats do come home on their own after an unexplained absence. Looking through years of case records of hundreds of missing cats, the number one way cats are found is that they simply come home in about twenty percent of missing cat cases. If your cat is going to come home on his own, looking for him, in the proper way, certainly won't hurt his chances of coming home. If your cat is one of the majority that don't simply come home of their own accord, then waiting to start the search could drastically reduce your chances of success. At a minimum, thoroughly check inside the house. About five percent of cats are found hiding in the house, having never left. You want to exclude this possibility before investing too much time and effort in other search strategies. Then you can get started on many aspects of the search that are best pursued early. You want to talk to the neighbors right away because memories fade and critical information could be lost if you wait.

3. Don't believe everything people tell you.

When you start talking to your neighbors, before you talk to your tenth neighbor, someone will have told you that your cat was killed by a predator and there is no point in looking. In every missing cat case I have worked, the owner was told by one or more people that a predator killed her cat. In Western Washington, people usually say a coyote killed your cat. This is somewhat unlikely, even though it does happen once in a while. Out of over a thousand carefully documented missing cat cases, fewer than three percent were proven to have been killed by predators. Over seventy percent of missing cats made it back home, one way or another. Misinformation like this is responsible for more cats not being found than actual deaths by predators. When distraught people hear stories of pets killed by predators and believe there is no hope, they stop looking. Death by predator can become a self-fulfilling prophecy when the cat owner stops looking and leaves the cat exposed to predation much longer than necessary. If you tell people your cat is missing, you will get all kinds of advice based on limited experiences and based on hearsay and rumors. One bit of advice passed around the internet is to urinate in a spray bottle and then spray your urine around the neighborhood to guide your cat home. I'm not making this up. Many people have tried it, against my advice, and I have seen zero evidence that it ever worked once. If you think about it, you would not smell like urine, in your cat's view. You would smell like you. Simply walking around your neighborhood looking for your cat is going to deposit your scent around the area. You don't normally pee all over your house or your yard, hopefully, so there is no reason why the scent of your urine would guide your cat home.

Another source of unhelpful information is the category of pet psychics or animal communicators. Is this a legitimate source of information? My answer is, obviously not. However, at least a quarter of the people who have sought my help disagreed with me and also sought the help of psychics and communicators. Whether or not I believe ESP to be legitimate, if it worked for some reason, I would be in favor of people using it. In all the hundreds of cases of which I have personal knowledge, none was ever solved because of information provided by a pet psychic or an animal communicator. However, I do know of instances where the psychic provided potentially harmful information, such as that a pet was deceased and the owner should stop looking. In some of those cases, the pet was alive and found because the owner ignored the psychic's advice. If you believe pet psychics and animal communicators are legitimate, then you probably won't be persuaded if I tell you otherwise. I hope you will believe me when I tell you such sources of information have never proven useful. If you do use a psychic, think about the types of information you are getting. My clients have been told things like, their pet is near water, or by a green house, or the cat is lonely and frightened, or the dog is happy and exploring. Even if any of that information was true and accurate, it wouldn't help you find your cat. Psychics often report seeing through the cat's eyes, but they never seem to be looking at a street sign or an address, or anything concrete and helpful. If you do hire a psychic or communicator, and you believe what they say, I urge you to set aside those visions and tips as one possible set of information. You can investigate those claims if you want, but don't let it guide your search. Consider information gathered in this way the same as you would consider a tip from a neighbor if they said they saw your cat in a certain place: you would check it out, but you wouldn't stop doing any of the other things you were doing based on a possible sighting that may or may not be your cat.

Yet another source of dubious information comes from people in my line of work who help search for lost pets in a volunteer capacity or as a profession. I have worked on many cases where the owner of the missing cat also sought help from another Pet Detective, Animal

Tracker, or a nonprofit group. At Missing Pet Partnership, where I volunteered and received my training, the advice we gave was based on documented experience of what worked and what didn't. Certainly we tried some things to see if they would work, but the only methods we recommended were the ones that had been proven to work in actual cases. Some of the information given by other organizations and individuals has been useful and accurate, and some has been harmful, mistaken, or ridiculous. How do you know that I am giving you the best advice? It can be difficult for an inexperienced person to judge. Ideally, there would be some regulating agency that would certify people in this business and give you some assurance that they have received the proper training and they abide by a code of ethics. I can show you my certificates documenting my training at Missing Pet Partnership, which is the most trusted organization specializing in finding lost pets. I can show you the awards I've won. However, I know of several people who have won awards and received certified training who are never the less giving bad advice to owners of missing cats. Whether you trust me is more than just a matter of personal and professional pride for me. It could make a huge difference in whether or not you find your cat. I hope to persuade you to follow my advice by presenting it in a clear and concise manner, and by impressing you with the amount of thought, time, experience, and effort that went into creating this guide. In the end, you need to be skeptical of all the advice you get on finding your lost cat, and you need to take a course of action that will optimize your chances of success without closing off any avenue of the possible return of your cat. It is a real problem for the cat owner, not knowing who to believe. I can't say I've never made a mistake. The advice I'm giving you here is similar to the advice you would get from Missing Pet Partnership, along with hints and tips based on my experience on hundreds of cases. I am constantly learning with each new missing cat case, and I try to tailor my advice to give each cat the best chance of coming home again. Please read through everything I've written here, and then compare it to the advice you get from other sources. I hope what I say makes sense and proves useful.

4. Don't call the name of a lost cat.

I am probably too late with this advice. By the time you read this, you probably will have already called for your cat. Sometimes it works. However, if it doesn't work, calling your cat's name could make the situation worse.

The reason calling your cat's name could be harmful is related to predator/prey relationships and instincts. I witnessed a small Screech Owl being mobbed by chickadees, humming birds, towhees, and warblers. He was just sitting there, trying to take an afternoon nap. The little birds pointed him out in order to warn others of his presence, but also in hopes of attracting a larger Barred Owl, which preys on the smaller Screech Owl. This scenario is played out with many different species of predators and prey. It is instinctive, not something they planned. When your cat is displaced from his home territory by some traumatic event, such as a cat fight, nearly being run over by a car, or being chased by a dog, he will probably act as a prey animal, trying to avoid the attention of predators. We've all seen our cats act as predators when they chase a laser dot or bring us the remains of a mouse. Cats instinctively know that they can become prey, as well. When your cat is hiding in silence, avoiding predators real or imaginary, the last thing he wants is for you to focus attention on him. When you call his name, he instinctively feels that you are shining a spotlight on him, pointing him out to any predators in the area, as in the example of the little birds calling attention to the Screech Owl. Calling your cat's name will probably increase his anxiety. Even if he wants to be with you, his fear of predators will outweigh his drive to come home, in most cases. In a few cases, calling a cat's name has worked, but given the potential for making things worse, you shouldn't risk it. There are other ways to attract him to you.

Instead of calling a cat's name, just talk to yourself in a casual tone of voice. You don't want to sound worried or anxious. You want to sound calm, so your cat can be calm. If you've ever spoken in an angry or agitated tone of voice at some person or thing in your house, perhaps even shouting at the TV, you may have seen your cats or dogs look worried, wondering if they ought to run and hide. Our pets pick up on our moods. You want to sound calm so that your cat can be calm. Some people want to express to their cats just how desperate they are to have them back home. While it's great that you want your cat home so passionately, that's not the message your cat is going to receive. He is going to think, *Mom is worried and anxious, so I should be worried and anxious. I'll stay hidden until it's safe.* Instead, even though it's a lie, you want to convey an attitude of, "It's fine if you stay hidden. You can come out if you want to, or not. I really don't care." If you feel self-conscious about wandering your neighborhood talking to yourself, then call someone on your cell phone and have a long, pleasant conversation with them.

Other things you can do instead of calling your cat's name include rattling his food bowl with a little kibble in it. Don't shake it continuously. Just rattle it once or twice a minute. You can also crinkle one of those packages that treats come in, if he is accustomed to getting those kinds of treats. If your cat lives with other cats, and if he knows their names because you say them often, then call the name of a cat that is safely at home. If you can record happy sounds of your other cats about to get their dinner, then you can play that recording on your smart phone as you walk around looking for the missing cat. You will not be focusing your attention on the lost cat, but you will be giving a familiar sound that your cat might associate with dinner time or extra attention.

5. Don't give up.

Many people who have hired my services, with or without a search dog, have put all their hopes into this one peak of activity. If the cat is not found in those days when we are trying everything we can think of, some people are unable to continue the search for a long period. Perhaps they are too busy, or it might be too stressful to always be in crisis mode while looking for a lost cat. In at least fifteen percent of missing cat cases, it took over three weeks for the cat to be found, finally. Those cats were found because the owners kept up their search. The rate of cats returning to their owners could be increased dramatically if only cat owners could have the patience and resolve to continue the search in a sensible way. Because of the way cats behave when frightened or displaced, it is not at all unlikely that a missing cat would be found weeks or months later. You may be told that searching for your cat is pointless, but experience has shown that the highest rate of return of missing cats goes to those families who follow the advice in this guide, and who don't stop looking.

Steps to take in the search for your missing cat. There are over a dozen typical pathways for a cat to return to his home. You want your actions to cover all those possibilities and give your cat the greatest possible chance of being found. When making a plan of action, you can be most effective if you make some tasks a priority. The actions listed below are usually best followed in the order listed. You can skip a step or rearrange the order if the particulars of your case warrant a different approach. For example, if you know that your cat was lost when he escaped a carrier between your car and the front door of the veterinary office, then there's no point in searching your home thoroughly. However, I urge you not to skip a step if you just don't like the suggestion or believe it would be useful. Many people have been skeptical of some of these methods until they witness their effectiveness in person. Also, keep in mind that each particular step, by itself, is unlikely to be the one key that brings your cat home. If you cover all the steps, or as many as you possibly can, you greatly increase your chances of finding your cat. In records of hundreds of cases of missing cats, there is a high degree of correlation with the willingness of people to follow all these steps and the people who end up finding their cats. These steps are guaranteed *not* to work if you don't try them.

1. Search thoroughly inside your house.

Every time I offer this bit of advice, I am told that the cat's owner already looked inside the house and is certain the cat is not there. In at least five percent of missing cat cases, they were wrong. One cat hid inside a wall for three weeks. One cat was in a dresser, behind the drawer. One suddenly appeared inside the house, and the owners never knew where he had been hiding. It is important that you thoroughly check every possible place, even if you don't believe your cat could fit in there. For one thing, many people will leave an exterior door open in hopes that their cat will come back in during the night. That's a good strategy, unless your cat was hiding somewhere inside the house. If your cat comes out of hiding and finds an open door, he may become truly lost at that point. Many people say, "I called my cat's name, and he didn't answer or come out, so I know he's not in the house." If a cat is injured, frightened, or sick, he will often hide in silence. Perhaps he would come to your voice under normal conditions, but many cats will change their behavior if they are not feeling well. In one case, a cat hid in a cupboard for nine weeks without food or water, and he survived when he was eventually discovered. The owner had no idea her cat was nearby the whole time. Use a strong flashlight to look under and inside things. If you have a cell phone that takes video, you can often stick your phone into tight, inaccessible places, with a flashlight, and record a video of the interior. I have found cats on cell phone video this way, when sticking my head into the space would have been difficult or impossible. Did you have the access to the attic or the crawlspace open recently? Have you looked in the rafters of the garage? Have you moved every box in the garage and looked behind it? Are there any openings in the drywall or behind the bathroom vanity? Was any remodeling being done around the time the cat disappeared? Even if you think these scenarios are unlikely, you need to eliminate these possibilities first.

2. Enlist help.

In some families, everyone is equally concerned about the missing cat. In other families, one person is particularly attached, and others in the family are less interested in helping, or unavailable. If you have family to help you, that's great. Make sure you put them to good use. Organize your search effort so that one person is coordinating all the communication, so that nothing is missed or duplicated. If you can't get the help you need from your family, reach out to other animal lovers near you. Some of your neighbors will be particularly concerned about a missing cat. Local businesses may be willing to display your posters for your missing cat. In Seattle, craigslist is a popular way to advertise your missing cat, and complete strangers may feel motivated to help you look. Not all cities make such good use of craigslist. You can get help on Facebook or a local blog. Also, you may find a volunteer group near you that specializes in helping find lost pets, or a professional company like Three Retrievers. You will also enlist help through fliers and large posters. When you recruit people to help you, make it as easy as possible for them to help. Get your search organized and have jobs ready that a helper could jump right into. Organize lines of communication so that work is not duplicated or overlooked. I have known individuals to put in 80 hours per week physically looking for their missing cat. It can be a large job, so try to spread the work over many helping hands, and don't do it all yourself if possible.

3. Keep a record of everything.

Take written notes, take pictures, and record voice notes if you can. On many searches for missing cats, the owner has received a tip about a potential sighting, gone to check it out, and found out that they can't find the cross streets or address of the sighting. In such a case, it may be critical to have contact information so you can call the person back and get better directions. When a member of your family is missing, you may not be getting as much sleep as usual, and you probably aren't eating properly. Your concentration may be diminished. Keep a notebook dedicated to this search, or use your smart phone to record everything. Make notes of the actions you have taken and make a list of the things that need to get done. When you are out looking for your cat, make note of any other missing cat fliers in your area. You may even wish to take a picture of any fliers you come across, for future reference. For one thing, a sudden rash of missing cat fliers in the area could provide a clue to what has happened to your cat. Also, you may wish to team up with the owner of the other lost cat. She can help look for your cat and you can help look for hers. Record the areas you have searched, and when you searched them. If you are handy with smart phone apps, you can have your phone record a map of everywhere you walked while searching. If you get sightings, be sure to record the locations and times as accurately as possible. If you see a pattern starting to develop, create a map showing these sightings, so you know where to place fliers and posters next. Keep track of the places you put up fliers and posters, so you can go back later and make sure they are still in good shape. Make a list of all the local shelters where your cat could possibly end up, and record when you visited each of them. If you hire someone to help you with your search, the more information you have available, the more he can help you. It is difficult to know in advance what little bit of information will prove vital down the road, so just assume that everything is important, and write it all down.

4. Understand lost cat behavior.

Your cat may act differently under stress, or if he is injured. Many people are surprised to learn that it is common behavior for a cat to hide in silence for seven to ten days when stressed or injured. Normally, your cat might come to you when you call, but you can't rely on that behavior now. In many cases, a missing cat was later found to be hiding nearby while the owners passed several times, calling the cat's name. I will discuss this tendency to hide in silence in more detail later, but the key point is that you need to account for the changes in behavior of lost cats. If you conduct your search based on your cat's usual behavior, you might just make matters worse, or miss opportunities. However, it is important to factor in your cat's usual behavior in order to prioritize some possibilities and decide which scenarios deserve less of your attention. Someone with more experience with lost cats can help you review your cat's behavior, personality, and physical traits, to come up with the best plan. Even if you don't have an experienced advisor, taking time to review your cat's traits can help you focus your search. A complete evaluation of your cat's behavior, physical attributes, and personality is beyond the scope of this book because there would be too many variables with all the different cats out there. However, taking a few moments to make note of your cat's traits can help you think about the likelihood of various scenarios later. The following is a list of questions I would ask someone when helping to find her cat. It is a long list, but it shouldn't take you too long to jot down the answers. Some of the questions may not apply to your cat.

Physical traits:

1. How old is your cat?
2. Spayed or neutered? Is she in heat? Has she been in heat recently?
3. Does he have a microchip? If so, have you contacted the microchip company to be certain your information is up to date?

4. Is he wearing a collar? Is it a breakaway type? How long has he had the same collar? What does the collar look like?
5. Is he wearing tags? Does the tag have your current number? Do the tags jingle?
6. How much does he weigh?
7. What does he look like? Long or short hair? Color? Distinguishing features?
8. Is he taking any medications right now? Does he have any physical problems? What is his past medical history? Has he had urinary tract infections in the past?
9. Has he been declawed?
10. Has he gained or lost weight recently?

Past behavior:

1. Is your cat indoor only? Indoor/outdoor? Outdoor only?
2. Does he like to hunt? Does he bring you intact birds and mice? Does he eat what he kills?
3. Has he gone missing before for any length of time? What happened then?
4. Do you have more than one cat? Do they get along well? Tolerate each other? Do they need to be separated because of constant fighting?
5. How does your cat behave around other cats in the neighborhood? Does he fight, play, or stay away?
6. Does he climb trees? Does he get over fences easily?
7. What does he do around dogs? Some cats will walk right up to dogs, while others run at the first sight of one.
8. Is your cat food motivated? Does he come running at dinner time? Does he show little interest in food?
9. Does your cat share a litter box with another cat? Have you added a new cat to your home recently?
10. Does your cat shed a lot or not very much? If possible, take a photograph of a place where your cat has rubbed against an edge and left fur.
11. Has your cat been trapped in a humane trap before?

Personality:

1. How would your cat behave if an unfamiliar person came into your house?
2. If you have guests, will your cat come out to see them eventually? How long does it take your cat to warm up to a person?
3. Does he sleep in your bed? Or in his own special place?
4. Is your cat nervous even around you?
5. Did your cat suffer any abuse or neglect in a previous home?
6. Does your cat like or dislike any particular type of person? Men vs. women. Kids or adults. Loud or quiet.
7. Has your cat's personality changed over time?

Environmental factors:

1. Is your neighborhood urban, suburban, or rural? What size is the average lot?
2. How old are the homes? Are there many homes with crawlspaces that may or may not be sealed?
3. Are there homes nearby that have a lot of junk or inoperative vehicles? Are there homes in disrepair?
4. Are there vacant or foreclosed homes? Are there any homes under construction?
5. If you live near woods or a greenbelt, how passable is it? Can you walk around through the underbrush? Are the brambles so thick that it is almost impossible to get through without a machete?
6. Are there water sources nearby? Streams or ponds?
7. Have there been any work vans or moving trucks that were open about the time your cat disappeared? Any RV's that were being aired out?
8. Has anyone gone on vacation recently?
9. Does your cat like to walk on the roof of your house?
10. Does anyone in the neighborhood use a humane trap for pest control? Is anyone poisoning rats?

11. Do you know of any particular neighbor with strong feelings against cats? People who feed birds or garden may be opposed to neighborhood cats coming into their yards.
12. Are there other fliers in your neighborhood for missing cats or small dogs?
13. Have there been any verified, witnessed incidents of cats or small dogs being killed by predators in the neighborhood? (Many people report that their cat was killed by a predator based on assumptions, not on fact.)
14. What are the roads like in your area? What are the speed limits? Are they usually obeyed?
15. How long has your cat lived at your current address? Where did you live before with him?
16. Is anyone feeding feral cats, their own cats, or wildlife at their back door?

Even if you can't do a thorough analysis of what all this data means when pieced together into a big picture, it still may be helpful for you to review this information when deciding on the highest priorities in your search. If you know your cat is very frightened of vehicles, you can put less emphasis on the possibility that your cat jumped into a moving van. It is still possible your cat climbed into a chest of drawers and was accidentally loaded onto a truck, but you may want to pursue other scenarios first. This type of information is better for solving the mystery of why your cat disappeared in the first place. Once your cat was displaced, his behavior may be much more similar to an average lost cat, regardless of his behavior and personality before the event.

Over seventy percent of lost cats are found. (The actual percentage may be higher, but not everyone answered our follow-up queries.) How did they behave during the time they were lost? We don't always know all the details, but information gained on hundreds of searches for missing cats can help you predict the behavior of your missing cat.

In reviewing the hundreds of cases where I have provided assistance, I can't find a single instance where the missing cat was found at the local shelter when the owner went to look there. You still need to check the shelter, as outlined in step 10 below, but it is unlikely that your missing cat will end up at the shelter, at least within the first two weeks. Why is that? How can it be that the shelter is full of cats, craigslist is full of ads for missing cats, and the cats at the shelter aren't the ones people are looking for? It is possible that people who found their cats at the shelter just never needed to contact me for assistance or place an ad for a lost cat. It may also be that most people aren't aware of the tendency of a frightened or injured cat to hide in silence for seven to ten days. People may look at the shelter during this hiding period, and then the cat ends up at the shelter after the owner has given up looking. The reasons vary from case to case, but most likely, your cat won't end up at the shelter right away for reasons related to the cat's behavior and the behavior of people.

Cats can hide in silence, without food or water, for seven to ten days. They will do this if they are frightened or injured, as an instinctive survival mechanism. Many cases have been documented of cats being trapped for weeks without food and water and surviving. The two longest cases I know of are seven weeks and nine weeks. If your cat was displaced from his home territory, and he hid in silence for a week or a month, he could be found after you've stopped going to the shelter and putting up fliers. I would hypothesize that shelters are full of cats because they end up there after people have stopped looking for them. A month or two is a long time to be worrying about the fate of your lost cat, as I know from experience. Many people will say, "I've done the best I can, and it's time to move on." I don't want you to be in agony and despair every day for weeks on end, with no end in sight. Instead of simply giving up or feeling the loss deeply every day, you can take a middle road where you acknowledge that you might not see your cat again but you leave the possibility open. When you visit the shelter for the fortieth time, you might think it is hopeless and pointless. However, many people who did not give up looking were rewarded for their efforts. One cat was found living two blocks away after he had been missing two months. Another cat was found living half a block away, six months later. The behavior of the cats and the behavior of the people who miss them can combine to reduce the chances of a reunion. Once you understand why that might happen, you can take steps to bridge that gap by not giving up. The number one reason people do not find their cats is because they give up.

Another factor that reduces the odds of your cat being at the shelter is that most people don't assume that a cat sitting on a fence or in someone's yard is a lost cat. Because cats often roam free, you can't just pick up every cat you see, assuming it is lost. This is good for the roaming cats, in a way, but it makes things difficult for the lost cat. Because outdoor access cats tend to roam at least a couple of houses away from home, people are conditioned to overlook a cat sitting in a yard, even if the cat is unfamiliar to them. Cats can also set up a new home if they are displaced. Every cat lover I know has had at least one cat where they said, "He just showed up one day, so we kept him when we were unable to find his owner." If many cats are acquired that way, it stands to reason that many cats would be lost in that same way.

If your cat is missing in a neighborhood with other outdoor cats, he could be displaced because of territorial disputes. If your cat was indoor only, then he is probably the low man on the totem pole when it comes to the outdoor world of cats. He could be intimidated or pushed around or injured by a smaller cat with more experience in outdoor cat games. If your cat had an established outdoor territory, a new cat in the area could have upset the established territories of the existing cats in the area, causing territories to shift. While you are looking for your cat, make note of the cats you see. If there is a new cat in the area that no one knows, pay particular attention to his actions and movements. He is likely the reason your cat is not coming home. In some cases, you may need to trap this new cat, and hold him temporarily, to give your cat a chance to come home or come out of hiding.

Of the cats that are eventually found, 90% are found within a block of home, and most of those were within five houses of home. Very few cats are found blocks or miles away. In rare cases, a cat will travel a mile or two to an old home. About 5% of cats were accidentally transported to a new area, across town or across the country. If your cat is more than two blocks from home, you aren't going to find him by driving around looking. You would find him by getting the attention of someone who has seen your cat. You should concentrate your search on every conceivable hiding place within a seven-house radius of your cat's known territory.

5. Protect yourself. You can't help your cat if you don't protect your health, safety, and peace of mind. When you seek help from a professional, from a volunteer group, or from a well-intentioned stranger, consider the source of the information you are getting. There are many people out there right now, making lots of money every day, telling cat owners stories that sound good. I know of at least two people with search dogs who just run their dogs a certain distance and never followed the scent trail at all. I know this because of my experience, both on cases and in training, of how scent trails work. I also know this because I have worked many of the same cases after these people have collected their money and gone, and it was highly unlikely that the missing cat could have traveled where they said, based on the evidence we found. For one thing, out of over 500 missing cat cases for which I have records, over 90% of the cats that were found ended up being within seven houses of home. If you hired a search dog and he supposedly followed the scent trail of your cat for five blocks, walking right down the sidewalk, ask yourself how likely it is that your cat would behave that way. It is certainly improbable, from a statistical point of view, for a lost cat to behave that way. If you do hire a professional to help you with a lost cat search, be sure you know what services you will be getting. If possible, contact someone who has used his or her services before. Also, keep in mind how you found out about a person or a service. For example, one person sends a spam email to every person on craigslist who is missing a pet. This is a direct violation of the terms of service for using craigslist. Ask yourself, if this person was willing to violate his agreement with craigslist to get your business, how ethical is he?

If you post ads about your missing cat on public forums like craigslist or Facebook, be prepared for at least one person to call you up and say horribly mean things. There may not be much you can do about it, but if you know in advance that some people like to cause distress to people who are already hurting, then it will at least come as less of a shock when you get one of these calls. People will say things like, "I ran over your cat," and much worse. While it is possible that someone did hit your cat with a car, it is unlikely, and you should be skeptical. If someone is calling from a blocked or unknown number, be skeptical from the start. Ask for a number where you can call the person back. If someone says he has your cat, and you should bring the reward money to a certain place, be especially cautious. It could be true, but it is most likely a con. After you've asked many questions, if you think this person could actually have your cat, don't go alone, and don't bring cash. Ask that they meet you in a well-lighted, busy public place.

Some people who are missing their cats will jeopardize their health and safety by simply searching non-stop. While I certainly recommend that you invest as much time as you can in searching the proper way, you need to take time out for your own health and safety. I have worked with people who were, really, cognitively impaired because they did not eat properly, they could not sleep, and they would not rest. People who would normally be very perceptive and have excellent recall can become scattered and unable to focus on the best course of action. If you search so hard and so long that you reach this state, you are doing your cat a disservice. You need to rest so that you can give your cat your best effort. Also, I have known people to take unnecessary risks as far as trespassing on private property or entering unsafe buildings and yards because they were desperate to find their cats. A lost or displaced cat is typically not going to move that quickly, so there will be time to get the proper permissions, and take appropriate safety precautions.

6. Print fliers.

This is something that most people do right away. Although it is number six on this list, you are still getting it done within the first 24 hours, hopefully. Most people have computers with printers, so as long as you have a good picture and your phone number on there, almost any sort of flier will work for the initial search. If you don't find your cat quickly, give some thought to making your next round of fliers as effective as possible. Ideally, you want to have your fliers direct people to a web page or Facebook page so they can get the latest information, no matter how old the flier is. You can do this by including a QR code, which is a common code used to direct people to web pages when they scan the code with an appropriate app on their smart phones. This is not hard to do. I have a standard way that I set up a web page, a Facebook page, and a flier so that they all link to each other. It takes me less than an hour to do this. It might take you more than an hour if it is the first time you have done these things. The flier directs people to the Facebook page and the web page. The Facebook page includes a picture of the flier, so people can print it out and share it. The Facebook page and the web page link to each other. Step by step instructions for making this type of flier can be found on the web site for Three Retrievers, www.3retrievers.com . Look on the Information page.

Generally speaking, you want your fliers to be simple and clean, easy to read. The picture on the flier should show the best view of your cat to help people identify him. If you have a funny picture of your cat wearing a costume, you might want to post that on your Facebook page, but don't use it for the only picture on your flier. The picture on your flier should be simple and clear, and show distinctive markings, if any, that will help people distinguish your cat from others.

These fliers are not a substitute for posters. The purpose of having the fliers is to distribute them quickly. Hand them to people out walking their dogs. Give a flier to the mail carrier, the garbage collector, the milk man, the paper carrier, and neighbors. A copy of your flier should be available at the local shelters your cat might show up at, and local veterinarians, especially those operating 24 hours. If possible, put up a flier in the nearest coffee shop, post office, pet store, and veterinary hospital. Encourage people to take a photo of the flier so the information will be available on their cell phones whenever they might need it.

If your fliers link to a web page and a Facebook page, you may wish to make half-page or quarter-page fliers so that they will go farther and last longer. When I am on a search with my dog, Komu, I like to have quarter-page fliers in my pocket so that I can hand something to someone quickly. Color copies can be expensive, and since most cats are black, white, or shades of gray, you can probably get by with black and white fliers. Save the expensive color pictures for your posters. The only time you really need to stick with color fliers is when the distinctive color of your cat is what will help someone distinguish your cat from a similar cat. If your cat is black, then there's no point in spending extra money on color fliers. If your cat was wearing a green collar, then you may wish to stick with color fliers because green, pink, and orange can all look the same in a black and white photo.

7. Mark the rear window of your car. Although high school students have been writing on car windows for decades, Kat Albrecht was the first person (as far as I know) to use this idea for missing pets. Missing Pet Partnership has an excellent description of this method on their web site. This is something I definitely recommend for a missing dog, but it can also be effective in some cases of missing cats. It doesn't cost much, and it certainly won't hurt to try it. The downside of this technique is that you will probably need to order the special markers online, so you may not be able to do it right away. In some areas, a police uniform supply store may carry these markers. They are Neoplex brand markers. If you use window makers from the grocery store or crafts store, they probably won't last very long and your message won't be as visible. Get at least three colors of markers. I usually use green, orange, and pink. Plan your letter spacing before you start. Use the tiny wires for your rear window defroster as a guide to keep your words straight. Use a few simple words, plus your phone number. An example would be: LOST ORANGE CAT GEORGETOWN 206-552-0304. You can also tape a picture of your cat to the rear window, inside a plastic sheet protector, next to the lettering. This inexpensive measure will catch the attention of people in a slightly larger circle as you go to the grocery store and to and from work. It is unlikely that your cat traveled more than a block from home, but it does happen once in a while. You want to cover all the possibilities in order to give your cat the best chances of being found. Keep in mind, when using Neoplex markers, that the ink will come off of your car window if you use window cleaner. It will not, however, come off your clothes, ever.

8. Ask the neighbors. Now that you have your rear window marked and your fliers printed, go door to door and talk to your neighbors. Be sure to give each of them a flier. In addition to asking if they know where your cat is now, ask if they have seen your cat in the past. Many people are surprised just how far their cats roam. They assumed it was just next door, and then someone four houses away will say they see him several times a week. Getting a better picture of your cat's territory can help you plan your search better. Here is a list of questions you would ask your neighbors, although the questions would vary, depending on if your cat was indoor-only, or wearing a collar or not, etc.

1. Do you know where my cat is right now?
2. Have you seen my cat at any time in the past several weeks (both before and after he went missing)?
3. Have you found his collar?
4. Have you had your garage door open or your shed doors open, and is it possible he is trapped in your garage or shed?
5. Do you know of any cats in the area that have gone missing recently?
6. Do you know of any new cats in the area that are unfamiliar?
7. Are there lots of cats roaming the neighborhood? Just a few? None?
8. Do you know of any neighbors that strongly object to cats in their yards? Do you know of anyone who is trapping animals?
9. Do you know of any neighborhood email lists or web pages or Facebook pages where I could post a notice of my missing cat?
10. Would you mind if I looked under your deck and under your shed with a flashlight?
11. Do you know of any work vehicles or moving vans or motor homes that were left open recently?

In case after case, I have uncovered new information just by asking. You would think that people would just see the flier for the lost cat on the telephone pole, as they are walking to get the mail, and just come forward with whatever they know. For some reason, many people withhold potentially useful information unless you ask them fairly specific questions. Maybe they don't think the information is relevant. Maybe they don't want to bother you if they can't tell you exactly where your cat is at this moment. Whatever the reason, someone in the neighborhood is very likely not telling you something about your cat. You need to be persistent with your questions if you want to give your cat the best chance of coming home. If you are reluctant to be this comprehensive and persistent with your neighbors, then try to find a friend, a volunteer, or a professional who will ask these questions for you. Keep in mind that as you ask these questions, some of your neighbors will tell you discouraging things, such as that your cat was probably killed by coyotes so there is no point in looking. You now know that it is very unlikely that a coyote killed your cat. You don't necessarily need to correct your neighbor, but try to get past that and find out if they know anything more relevant to your search.

9. Create large neon posters. Many people feel that 8.5 by 11 inch fliers on the telephone poles are adequate. They are not. People ignore these fliers, mostly. Sure, people like me will pull over and get out of the car to read a lost pet flier, but most people will just keep driving. If you make your posters right, people will read your posters whether they want to or not. They will see the large neon sign, designed to catch their attention. In seconds, before they are even aware of it, they will have read the important parts of the sign: REWARD—LOST CAT—206-552-0304. It would take more effort to *not* read that sign than to read it. Now, this person is thinking about cats. Missing Pet Partnership has an excellent page on their web site explaining why these signs work and how to make them. I definitely suggest you visit that page. You can see an example of the sign at www.3retrievers.com. A brief description of how to make them follows.

1. Purchase large poster paper, 22"x28", at your local grocery store or art supply store. Stick with yellow, green, and pink. The deeper colors don't catch the eye as well. While at the store, purchase two 8.5"x11" sheet protectors for every poster you will make. You also need a fat marker and some clear tape. You should make at least ten of these signs. You want enough signs so that no one could possibly come within two blocks of your home without being aware of your missing cat. An

excellent substitute for this colored paper is corrugated plastic available at most hardware stores. It costs more, but may be less expensive in the long run because it last longer.

2. Tape the sheet protectors in the middle of your vertically aligned poster board. Tape the openings down, to keep the rain out. Be sure not to interfere with the opening when taping the sheet protectors on. In one sheet protector, put a large, clear, sharp picture of your cat. This should be a simple picture, with no distractions such as family members, costumes, or odd expressions or postures. In the other sheet protector, put your phone number in 100 font or larger, big enough to read from fifteen feet away. Also include a brief description of your cat, such as WHITE, WITH BLACK COLLAR, or, SIAMESE WITH EXTRA TOES. Tape the openings closed with just a small tab of tape, just to keep the papers from sliding out.

3. Using the marker, write across the top, REWARD, in thick, bold letters. Plan out your spacing with light pencil marks, so the lettering looks as good as it can. Across the bottom: LOST CAT.

4. You can stop there, or you can beef up your posters by taping sturdy cardboard to the back. If you are anticipating calm, dry weather, you can probably skip the cardboard, but if you are expecting rain and wind, the cardboard backing will help the posters last much longer.

Placing your posters properly is the next step. If you are getting them up quickly, you might tape a few to sign posts temporarily. Many municipalities discourage signs on public sign posts and utilities. As soon as you can, get your signs onto private property by asking key property owners for permission. You want to place your sign near the intersection with the stop sign or traffic light. Ask the property owners at that intersection for permission to place your sign on a stake in his yard. Angle your signs so they are easily read from the street. Maintain them, and replace any that are lost or damaged. Drive in and out of your neighborhood a couple of times and make sure that no one can get in or out of your neighborhood without seeing one of your signs.

10. Check the shelters. You probably don't need to check the shelters on the very first day. It is a little unlikely that your cat would end up at the shelter that quickly, unless he was deceased and someone called animal control. You can wait until the second day to start checking shelters. Depending on where you live, you may need to check several shelters in the area. For example, if you lived in White Center, near Seattle, you would need to check the Seattle Shelter on 15th Ave, the King County Shelter in Kent, and the Burien shelter. Your cat could enter a new jurisdiction just by walking a block or two, in some cases. Someone could misunderstand the boundaries and take your cat to the wrong shelter. In the case of accidental transport, your cat could be miles away. Just to be safe, you should check with all the shelters within fifty miles. In my case, that would be at least ten shelters. You don't need to check the shelter every day. I would do it every other day, and you could go as long as every third day.

In the hundreds of cases of missing cats that I've worked on, I can't recall a single instance where the owner went to the shelter and found their cat. It probably happens. Maybe people who find their cats at the shelter never end up calling me for help. Why are there so many cats at the shelter and yet it is unlikely that you will find your cat at the shelter? I don't know for sure, but I suspect the main reason is that cats finally wind up at the shelter after their owners have given up looking. Animal Control Officers don't just drive around looking for cats to grab. In general, they would only take a cat if someone called and reported a stray in their neighborhood. If your cat is missing and gets displaced from his territory, he may get bumped along from one cat's territory to the next until he is a block or two away. Your cat could be living two blocks away without your knowledge. Maybe he eats at someone's back door for a month or two, and then he gets bumped into a new territory where the homeowner reports him as a stray. Another reason that your cat might not end up at the shelter right away would be if someone found him dirty and skinny and assumed he was abandoned, neglected, or abused. Even if you took the best possible care of your cat, he could look bedraggled after a week or two in hiding. Someone might give such a cat a new home, rationalizing to herself that the previous owners don't deserve to have their cat back. Some people don't want to send a cat to the shelter because of the depressing statistics about the number of cats that die in shelters every year. Whatever the reason, I just don't hear of many instances where the owner of the missing cat located him at the local shelter. That doesn't mean you shouldn't check. It is still possible he could be there. Certainly make sure they have your flier in their records. The most important time to check the shelters for your lost cat is during the time period from one month to a year after your cat goes missing. Most people give up before then. I know from experience that it can be hard to go to the shelter every day and see all those dogs and cats who need homes. I ended up with a couple extra cats and a new dog that way.

You can find your lost cat in one of approximately fifteen different ways. Each individual way of finding your cat is unlikely, by itself. The most common way of finding your cat, when he just comes home on his own, only happens less than 20% of the time. You maximize your chances of finding your cat by covering all fifteen possible ways he could be found. Look at it another way: if your cat is in your neighborhood, which is statistically the most likely case, he could be in any one of fifty different yards. There are forty different garden sheds he could be under, and sixty different decks he could be under. Maybe there are 100 trees he could be hiding in. When you look in one particular tree, the odds of finding him there would be less than one in 200, a very slim chance. Does that mean you shouldn't look in that tree if it is unlikely you would find him there? No, it means you need to look in all 100 trees, under all 60 decks, and under all 40 garden sheds in order to maximize your chances of finding your cat. So, even if it is a little unlikely that you will find your cat at the shelter on this particular day, you still need to go look.

11. Look in the right places at the right times. We've already started to address this. For example, you need to keep checking the shelters for up to a year, not just in the first few weeks. When and where you should look for your cat is dependent on his past behavior, his personality, and his environment and circumstances. If your cat is an indoor-only cat who just escaped, check in your neighbor's garage or

crawlspace. Don't look for him two blocks away. If your cat is a gregarious cat with a large known territory, then expand your search sooner. A good time to look for cats is at night, using a strong flashlight to check for eye reflection under cars, in shrubs, and up trees. Another good time to look for your cat is when the neighborhood is very quiet, between two and five AM. Go around at this time and remain quiet, without talking or calling your cat's name. Even if you don't see your cat, make note of the cats you do see. Are all of them accounted for? Does each one have a home? If there is a new stray cat in your neighborhood, then that could be the reason your cat doesn't come home.

One of the best times to look is when you aren't there at all, by way of a wildlife camera, discussed below. Given all the variables of all the different types of cats in different situations, it is difficult for me to make generalizations about the best time and place to look for your cat. That's why I like to do a one hour consultation with someone, to learn all I can about the cat before giving specific advice. Some generalizations I can make are: don't drive around for blocks looking for your cat on the first day he disappeared; do concentrate your search within seven houses of your cat's known territory; look at many different times of day; use technology to enhance your search; and get the help of family, friends, neighbors, and workers who pass through your neighborhood.

12. Use social media and internet tools. It is very likely that someone knows something about your cat. You just haven't made that connection yet. The internet is all about connections.

1. Craigslist. In the Seattle area, craigslist is used heavily for missing pets. In other cities, it is hardly used at all for this purpose. In those cities, there may be an alternative forum serving this function, but I don't know what it is. When using craigslist in a city where it is actively used for lost pets, take a few steps to ensure your ad is effective. Place your ad in the Lost & Found section. You can also place a second ad in the Pets section. According to craigslist rules, you should only place one ad every seven days. I understand the purpose of this

rule—to keep one person from flooding the listings with his ad for junk for sale. However, this rule can make it difficult to let people know about your missing cat. To get around this rule, without violating the spirit of the rule, you can make additional ads for your cat using a slightly different title and rearranging the words. Don't place more than two ads per day. One person places five or ten ads for her lost dog every day. I certainly sympathize with her need to find her dog, but she has generated backlash and drawn criticism for her overzealousness. Be sure your ad has some good, sharp, clear pictures. Include in your ad a link to the web page you have set up for your cat. Be aware that spammers sift through craigslist for email addresses to spam, so you probably want to use the craigslist email process and avoid giving out your personal email address. Also be aware that people will call you to offer pet-finding services, in a direct violation of the posted craigslist rules. If companies are willing to blatantly ignore the craigslist rules, you might wonder about their ethics.

2. Facebook. If you are on Facebook anyway, why not use it for something useful for a change? Some people spread the word about their missing cats simply by sharing on their own pages. That's fine and I certainly recommend that. However, if you create a separate Facebook page dedicated to your cat, you will find that people are more willing to share the page than if it was just a mention of your cat on your page. One missing dog had 500 likes on her Facebook page in just two weeks, and those Facebook connections eventually lead to her recovery. Other pages dedicated to missing pets have only generated 25 likes, or so. Even if those pages aren't as effective as the dog's page with 500 likes, it is a free service, and it takes you very little effort to give it a try. The key to success with a Facebook page is getting people to share it. You actually need to ask people, "Please share this page."

3. Pet Harbor. This is a web page that posts pictures of all the pets in a particular shelter. Not all shelters participate. Enter your

zip code and see if the shelter serving your area is listed. Also, it is not a substitute for going to the shelter in person and looking. However, if you just can't make it to the shelter today, it only takes a moment to look online for any new cats that have come in and been photographed. Pet Harbor would be great if all shelters participated.

4. Petfinder. This web site lists pets available for adoption from rescue agencies. In a perfect world, your cat would not end up at a rescue group—your lost cat is supposed to go to the local shelter, which operates under a different set of rules. Many cats do end up at rescues, somehow. If my cat were missing, I would look through the listings of local rescues and make sure he didn't end up being offered for adoption. It takes very little effort to check these listings. Just type in your zip code.

5. Twitter. Personally, I hate Twitter. I find it annoying and useless. I have made several attempts to like Twitter, but I can't get over the feeling that it is just stupid. Other people love Twitter and use it all the time. If you are one of those people who likes or tolerates Twitter, then it costs you nothing to publicize your missing cat through this channel. If nothing else, use Twitter to direct people to your Facebook page for your cat.

6. Shelter web pages. Some shelters that don't participate in Pet Harbor's program will have their own online photographs and listings of found or stray cats. Unfortunately, they don't all use any sort of standardized format. You just have to dig into each shelter's web page and search for listings of found cats. Sometimes, these listings are not very easy to find. Again, checking a shelter's web page is not a substitute for looking in person. Sometimes, a volunteer is in charge of posting the pictures on the web, and you can't be assured that your cat didn't fall through the cracks somehow.

7. MPP site. I volunteered for Missing Pet Partnership for four years, and MPP's Founder, Kat Albrecht, taught me most of what I know. I highly recommend looking through this web site. Much of the information provided here is also available on MPP's web site. My main reason for creating this handbook is just to gather the information into one package for convenience

of delivery. Also, I have added ideas and tools based on my own years of experience. Many of the ideas I am presenting here are explained in a slightly different way on the MPP site, and you might benefit from hearing things explained in a different way. I certainly don't disagree with anything you would read on the MPP site.

8. Neighborhood watch email lists, web pages, or Facebook pages. Hopefully, your neighborhood has a neighborhood watch group. Some people have gotten the word out about their missing cats very quickly and effectively by using this email list or web page. If your neighborhood is blessed with an absence of crime, your neighborhood watch group might not be active. Ask around and see if there is one in your area. Even if it is not a formal, established group, sometimes neighbors keep in touch through email, so try to get your cat's information circulated in this way. Type the name of your neighborhood into Facebook's search box, and see if there is a page dedicated to your area, or to a local park, or a local business.

9. Property records. In order to search all of the properties in your neighborhood, you first need to figure out who owns the property, which can be a challenge in some cases. King County, in which Seattle is located, has a very easy way of searching their database to find out who owns what property. You can just point to a place on a map, or you can type in an address. Other counties are not as easy to search. If there is a vacant lot, or a foreclosed home, publicly available property records may be the best way of determining who to contact. In an area like Seattle, this is really very easy.

10. Local blogs. The West Seattle Blog has a section devoted to missing pets. They are responsible for many happy reunions. Other local blogs don't have a dedicated section for lost pets, but they will post an article about your lost cat if you specifically ask them to. Again, if you can give them a link to your cat's web page or Facebook page, this blog posting is going to be more

effective. If all else fails, purchase a banner ad on your local blog. They won't say no to that.

11. Online pet sales (if your cat is exotic or valuable in some respect). The Seattle Times offers pets for sale in their classified section. I think this is deplorable because it is a sales tool for puppy mills and backyard breeders. True breeders, who follow the guidelines of the AKC and only breed dogs and cats for the improvement of the breed, don't advertise in the classifieds. Anyway, until these forums for pet sales are shut down, it is a way to monitor local sales of cats of your breed, if your cat is a purebred or exotic. If your cat is just a typical tabby or ordinary orange cat, then it is unlikely he would be seen here.

12. A blog page for your cat. As mentioned above in the section on making fliers, you can and should create a dedicated blog page for your missing cat. If you already have a blog page with an established base of readers, you can leverage that audience to build the audience of your cat's blog page. I have been using Blogger for years, and I find it simple and easy to use. Use the company that works best for you. If you are not comfortable setting up a blog page, perhaps you have a son or niece that can do it for you. Three Retrievers Lost Pet Rescue will also help you with this, if you like. Once the page is set up, you need to share it and link it to other pages. Have a link to your blog page within your craigslist ad.

13. Use a cat-detection dog, if available.

When people hear of a dog that finds lost cats, many people think the search dog is going to follow a scent trail to the hiding place where their cat has been ensconced, and they will know for sure where their cat is. Unfortunately, that is not how dogs find lost cats (in most cases), and it is important that you know why, before you hire a search dog to look for your missing cat.

Search dogs can and do follow the scent trails of missing *dogs* as they run in fear or go off exploring. Dogs tend to run many blocks or many miles when they disappear, and they leave a scent trail from point A to point B. Cats behave differently when they roam or flee. Even the most adventurous cat will usually stick to known paths and familiar territory. Mostly, cats move a little way, stop and leave a scent pool, move a little farther, and make another overlapping scent pool. What you are left with is not a scent trail from point A to point B, but a series of directionless pools of scent. Because individual cat trails are difficult or impossible to follow, we teach our cat detection dogs to find any cat they can. They are methodically searching areas of high probability, under our direction, looking for any cat they can find. The cat detection dog will become alert and excited when entering a pool of cat scent, and she will go nuts when she approaches the position of a hidden cat. If she finds a cat other than the one we are seeking, we tell her, "Good girl, go find another," and give her a treat reward.

Although the cat detection dog almost always finds some cats on a typical search, it is unusual for the dog to directly find the cat we are seeking during the typical three-hour search. Most of the time, we leave the owner's neighborhood without finding the cat we are looking for. This doesn't mean the cat wasn't there, necessarily, because we may have dislodged the cat from his hiding place when the search dog approached. In about a quarter of our cases, the cat was found shortly after we searched, and this may be because the missing cat came out of hiding when the dog approached. (All our cat-detection dogs are friendly with cats, but the cat doesn't know that.) In less than 20% of our searches does the search dog find the hidden cat directly, or remains of a deceased cat.

Why would you want to hire a search dog if the odds of immediate success are less than 20%? There are several reasons, and you should consider these factors when deciding whether a search dog is worth the time and expense.

- Value of a thorough search on neighboring properties.

- Attract attention to search.
- Know where cat is not
- Find evidence of predation.
- Search is not a substitute for everything else that needs to be done.
- Other tools used during the search.
- The value of experience with many searches.

When your cat is missing, you suddenly get to know neighbors that you have lived near for years but you've never really talked to them. I know this from my personal experience of losing a cat. You want to search your neighbor's property very thoroughly, but it feels awkward to say, "I wasn't all that interested in talking to you for the last eleven years, but now I want to snoop around your tool shed." Also, your neighbor may say he has checked his garage and your cat is not there when in fact your cat may be well hidden inside the garage. When you hire a cat-detection dog to do a thorough search, we are a disinterested third party. It feels less awkward for the cat owner and the property owner when a professional with a trained dog comes to do a thorough search. This way, it doesn't feel like you are poking your nose in your neighbor's business. We are just looking in those hiding places of highest probability. Also, the junk in one person's back yard looks much the same as the junk in another person's back yard, and we aren't making any judgments about the property owner. We are just looking for the lost cat. Having this search done by professionals makes it easier for everyone.

Another value of the search dog team is that it draws attention to the case of your missing cat. At least once a month, there is a new flier for a lost pet on the telephone poles in my neighborhood. I stop to look because that is my area of interest, but most people just cruise on by these fliers without paying much attention. Hopefully, if your cat is missing, you have bombarded your neighborhood with fliers and signs so that no one within a three-block radius could possibly be unaware of your missing cat. Even if you have done a good job with posters and fliers, the presence of a search dog team raises the level of awareness. It involves people in the search, gets them excited and motivated, and elicits useful information even when people have seen the posters and fliers. In many cases, the search dog team will get a critical tip from a neighbor. We feel like asking, "Well, why didn't you come forward with this information when you first saw the missing cat flier?" For whatever reason, the search dog gets people talking and draws out more and better tips. Some of these leads are mistaken or not actionable, but it provides more information that the cat owner can act on.

If the search dog leaves after three hours of looking, and your cat has not been found around the twenty homes closest to your house, you will at least know that your cat is not in that zone of highest probability. It is possible he moved out of his hiding place as the search dog moved through, but you know he is not hiding under the Wilson's shed or in the Johnson's garage. This not only allows you to stop worrying about those possibilities, it lets you focus your search on the next most likely scenarios. Cats do occasionally hitch a ride out of their neighborhood in a moving van or get locked inside a vacant house for sale. These are not as likely as simply hiding under the neighbor's shed, but such scenarios become more likely when you rule out the most likely situations. An effective search for a cat involves ruling out all the places your cat is *not*. You need to verify that your cat is not at the local shelter, not at the local vet, not just hiding under the bed, and not in the rafters of the neighbor's barn. You can rule out most of those places yourself. You can even do a thorough search of your neighbor's property without a search dog. It's just a lot easier and more effective if you bring in the search dog.

Another advantage of the search dog is that her nose can point out signs of predation that a human would overlook. This has happened in many cases. The possibility that your cat was taken by a coyote or another predator is one of the least likely things that could have happened. We keep records of the searches we perform, and their outcomes. We don't always know the final outcome, so our statics are incomplete. However, we can come up with a minimum and maximum probability of death by predator, accounting for the missing data, and so far the number of pets lost to coyotes and other predators is between 3% and 7%. Almost every other possibility—being at the shelter, hiding under a shed, being stuck inside the wall, hopping in a moving van—is more likely than being taken by a predator. Still, it does happen from time to time, and the search dog has found physical evidence where humans have passed many times without noticing. In four recent cases where we know a coyote took the pet, evidence of a kill was found within a hundred yards of the pet's house. If we do a thorough search of the areas of highest probability in your neighborhood and the search dog does not find any evidence of predation, then you can say that the likelihood is even lower than the average of 3% to 7%. You can concentrate on other possibilities and spend less time thinking your cat has been killed by a coyote.

A search dog is just one tool, and not a substitute for all the other ways of finding a lost cat. It wouldn't make sense to only post fliers on the doors of houses with odd numbers and not the even-numbered houses. Neither would it make sense to only hire a search dog if you don't plan on checking the shelters, posting the fliers, visiting the vet, and all those other useful techniques. The use of a search dog is most likely to be helpful when used in conjunction with all other avenues of discovery. Likewise, a visit to the shelter won't find your cat if he's still hiding in a tree in the neighbor's back yard. Your goal in your search for your cat is to check the most likely places first, and then do a thorough search of every place your cat could be. The search dog team covers those aspects of the search that an unaided human could not do as easily or as well.

Because the search dog is just one tool, the handler may bring other equipment on the search. We can bring listening devices to hear faint sounds in crawlspaces and in hedgerows. We have fiber optic scopes to look in crevices and around corners. We will have high-powered flashlights to detect eye reflection in crawlspaces. If predation is suspected, we have forensic chemical tests to help determine if the evidence is relevant to your case. Most of all, the MAR Technician handling the dog and guiding the search has the experience of hundreds of other searches, plus training specific to this situation. You should not be an expert in finding lost cats because, hopefully, it doesn't happen to you very often. You don't learn brain surgery just in case someone in your family might have a tumor, and most people aren't experienced with plumbing repairs because it is simpler and more effective—and often cheaper—to have a professional handle situations that come up rarely or never. We know what works and what doesn't when you are searching for a lost cat. Many web sites have free advice that is generally useful in finding a missing cat, but the handler that comes with the search dog can usually answer questions specific to your case because he has experienced the same situation with someone else's lost cat. Many of the techniques commonly employed by inexperienced people to find a lost cat are unhelpful, and some do more harm than good. We can guide you to the most effective methods and steer you away from ways that have failed in the past.

When you should probably *not* hire a search dog:

- If you can't get permission to search a majority of private property in the area of highest probability.
- If you aren't willing to take all the other steps necessary beyond the search with the dog.
- If your cat has been missing for over a month and there have been no reported sightings.
- If you haven't done a thorough search inside your house, including places your cat wouldn't normally go.
- If you don't have a reasonable understanding of what a search dog can and cannot do.

Toward that last point, this information is provided so that you don't have unrealistic expectations of the search dog, and so that you get the most out of your time and money, with the highest chances of success. Every case is different, so be sure to ask questions of the search dog handler before he comes out to work the dog.

You should also understand the physical limits of the search dog. He can only smell what he can smell. The abilities of a dog's nose are amazing, and a thousand times more powerful than the human nose. However, if the wind is blowing the wrong way, or if the conditions are too hot and dry, a search dog can walk right by a hidden cat without knowing it. We try to minimize the risk of this failure by searching in the best weather conditions (cool and moist) and accounting for wind direction. Still, on many cases, I have had a proven search dog walk along oblivious to a cat that we humans can plainly see fifteen feet away. This is not a failure on the part of the search dog. First of all, she is supposed to be using her nose, not her eyes. Second, dogs can't really identify objects that aren't moving: if I throw my dog's favorite orange ball onto a green lawn while she is not looking, that ball is almost invisible to her eyes and she must use her nose to find it. If her ball is moving, she can spot it from a mile away. Cats instinctively know that they become invisible to dogs if they hold still. It is the job of the search dog handler to work the search pattern with the wind flow to give the dog a chance to smell those cats, seen and unseen. Also, dogs can't climb trees or jump into the rafters of a garage, so the search dog may indicate the presence of a cat without being able to pinpoint the location of the cat. Dogs also lose interest in a game after a certain amount of time, so we usually limit the search to three hours, depending on the weather conditions and how the dog is holding up. I can't push a dog to search. She has to do it because she enjoys the game. The search dog is an amazing tool, but she has her limits, and the person relying on the search dog needs to be aware of those limitations.

Knowing everything I know about search dogs, I would certainly want the services of one if my cat were missing. When my cat did go missing in 1997, I wish I had been able to use the services of a professional with a detection dog. As helpful as we can be at times, we work best when the owner of the missing pet has a clear understanding of what we can and cannot do. I hope that we can help you.

14. Use a vocal cat to attract a missing cat. This isn't a technique I would recommend in every case. If you suspect your cat is hiding in the blackberries in the ravine behind your house (which happens often enough) then you may get him to come home if he hears another cat talking. Ideally, this would be another cat that he lives with. You would put the cat who is not lost in a secure crate and set the crate in the back yard. You would retreat to the house and keep an eye on the crate from a distance. In some cases, the missing cat has been attracted to

the cries of the crated cat. It doesn't always work, and it won't work if your cat isn't even in the bushes there, but it is just another technique to be aware of. An alternate version of this method is to make an audio recording of the cat who is not missing. Using your smart phone or other recording device, record the cat who is still at home when he is yowling in anticipation of dinner. Then, as you look around your neighborhood, play this recording from time to time and see if you get a reaction.

15. Consider an automated calling service. These services use automatic dialers to call every number within a certain radius of your home. I don't have much evidence to suggest this method is successful, but it is another avenue you can try if you want to be sure you are doing everything you can. Web sites that offer this service indicate which cats were found, but they usually don't mention if the cat was found specifically because of the calling service, or by some other method. If you use this method (I would if my cat was missing, just to cover all the bases) be aware that not all of these companies deliver what they promise. Recently, many of my clients have complained that a certain company did not send faxes to all the people they said they would. When my clients have used FindToto.com, I know that the phone calls were actually made because people we ran into told us they knew about the missing cat because of the call from FindToto. There may be others that are very reliable, but I don't have firsthand knowledge of them.

16. Use a wildlife camera. Special cameras are designed to be used by hunters so they can keep track of the movements of deer. The cameras are designed to sit out in the weather, and they take a picture of anything that triggers the motion sensor. The cameras I recommend have an infrared flash that uses light beyond the range that animals and people can see. This way, the cat is not frightened away by a blinding flash of white light. Wildlife cameras are useful in many situations. You can use one to see if your cat is in a particular area, and you can also use the camera to establish your cat's behavior patterns if you know for sure he is in an area but he is being evasive. Also, if the wildlife camera

just tells you what other cats are coming to the food, that can be helpful, too. I like to set up the camera so that it faces a wall or a fence, so the background is static and uniform. It takes pictures most reliably in this configuration. Set a plate of wet food or tuna near the wall, and place the camera about four feet away. You can just set the camera on the ground in most cases, or you can strap it to a post or a tree. You see what pictures the camera took by removing the memory card and placing it in your computer or digital camera. The pictures will have a time and date stamp on them. Once you establish that your cat is showing up, and you know what time, then you can proceed with trapping or luring methods. If your cat does not show up on camera after a couple of days, make note of what cats were photographed, and move your camera to a new location. I have had the best luck with Moultrie infrared cameras. Bushnell cameras have also worked okay. Some other brands have not worked at all for me, but maybe I just got a lemon. Three Retrievers Lost Pet Rescue rents out cameras in the Seattle area, or you can buy one through Amazon, Walmart, or Cabelas.

17. Set a humane trap. I don't recommend just setting a trap for every missing cat. You need to have a reason to believe your cat is in the area, first, which is why I recommend people start with the wildlife camera. When using a humane trap, you need to commit to checking it frequently, so that your cat, your neighbor's cat, or a wild animal isn't trapped too long. Especially if it is very cold or very hot, you need to check it often. If the temperature is over 80 or under 32, you probably shouldn't use the trap at all unless you are on hand at all times, watching it from a distance.

A humane trap is a metal wire cage with a door that falls shut when the cat steps on a trigger mechanism. I have trapped many cats and dogs, and the only minor injuries were to the noses of some feral cats when they bashed into the wall of the trap trying to get out. If used properly, it is very safe. The quality of traps varies considerably. You might have success with a trap you can get at your local hardware store. Three Retrievers has invested in TruCatch traps, which offer the best function and durability, in my experience. I rent these traps in the Seattle area.

If you catch a cat that isn't yours, don't just automatically release him. First, find out where he belongs. If he is a truly feral cat, then he might benefit from a trip to the vet, as long as you've got him captured. In several cases, trapping and temporarily removing a feral cat from the area allowed the missing cat to come home. Once your cat is home, you can release the feral cat back into the area after you have made sure he is neutered. If you catch a neighbor's cat, ask if they can keep him indoors for a couple of days. They might say No, but it doesn't hurt to ask. Explain that their cat may be interfering with getting your cat home. If you catch a wild animal, just be a little careful when you release it. If it's a skunk, wear a disposable plastic poncho when you open the trap. If it's a raccoon, don't be too nervous if it snarls at you. He will most likely run away when you open the door. Wear thick gloves just in case.

Generally speaking, it doesn't hurt to deploy a humane trap if you monitor it frequently. Preferably, you would set a wildlife camera to watch your trap, so you would know if your cat came up to the trap but wouldn't go in. The variations on using traps are too many to go into here. I could write a book on trapping alone. If you are going to use a humane trap, I would be happy to consult with you by phone and email to make sure you have the best chances of success. In addition to the humane trap, there are also drop traps and clam traps, and you can even use your house as a trap in some circumstances. Please take advantage of my years of experience with trapping, and don't hesitate to ask questions if you don't understand something.

In conclusion, I want to reiterate that you should not put all your hopes in one single method. If you just go to a shelter to look for your cat, and try nothing else, you are severely reducing your chances of success. If you just hire a search dog and try nothing else, you are not giving your cat the best chance of being found. If you follow all the steps given here, I would estimate that you have an 80% chance of finding your cat. One thing that applies to everything in this booklet: Don't give up. You will want to give up at some point because it feels hopeless. If you can work through that phase, you can get out of the emergency state of mind you had when your cat first went missing and settle into the long search effort. I know people who have invested hundreds of hours looking for their pets and been rewarded. Unfortunately, I also know a few who have spent hundreds of hours looking over many months and were never successful. At least 70% of people who sought my help found their pets, one way or another. People who diligently followed my advice (or Missing Pet Partnership's advice) found their pets about 80% of the time. People who, for whatever reason, did not follow the advice offered here, had significantly lower success rates. We are here to help, so please contact me if you have any questions or need further assistance.

Three Retrievers Lost Pet Rescue
www.3retrievers.com
206-552-0304
Jim@3retreivers.com

Made in United States
Troutdale, OR
06/18/2024